Seeds of Hope
Bereavement and Loss Activity Book

Helping Children and Young People
Cope with Change Through Nature

CAROLINE JAY

ILLUSTRATED BY UNITY-JOY DALE

Jessica Kingsley *Publishers*
London and Philadelphia

First published in 2015
by Jessica Kingsley Publishers
73 Collier Street
London N1 9BE, UK
and
400 Market Street, Suite 400
Philadelphia, PA 19106, USA

www.jkp.com

Copyright © Caroline Jay 2015
Illustrations copyright © Unity-Joy Dale 2015

All rights reserved. No part of this publication may be reproduced in any material form (including photocopying of any pages other than those marked with a ✓, storing it in any medium by electronic means and whether or not transiently or incidentally to some other use of this publication) without the written permission of the copyright owner except in accordance with the provisions of the Copyright, Designs and Patents Act 1988 or under the terms of a licence issued by the Copyright Licensing Agency Ltd, Saffron House, 6–10 Kirby Street, London EC1N 8TS. Applications for the copyright owner's written permission to reproduce any part of this publication should be addressed to the publisher. Warning: The doing of an unauthorised act in relation to a copyright work may result in both a civil claim for damages and criminal prosecution.

All pages marked ✓ may be photocopied for personal use with this programme, but may not be reproduced for any other purposes without the permission of the publisher.

Library of Congress Cataloging in Publication Data
Jay, Caroline, 1953-
  Seeds of hope, bereavement, and loss activity book : helping children and young people cope with change through nature / Caroline Jay ; Illustrated by Unity-Joy Dale.
     p. cm.
  ISBN 978-1-84905-546-8 (alk. paper)
  1. Death--Juvenile literature. 2. Bereavement--Juvenile literature. 3. Loss--Juvenile literature. 4. Loss--Juvenile literature. I. Dale, Unity-Joy. II. Title.
  HQ1073.3.J39 2015
  155.9'37--dc23
                    2014015362

British Library Cataloguing in Publication Data
A CIP catalogue record for this book is available from the British Library

ISBN 978 1 84905 546 8
eISBN 978 0 85700 970 8

Printed and bound in China

Hi,

Maybe you're reading this because someone you know has died or because your Mum and Dad are getting divorced or because someone has moved away or because there's been some other kind of loss in your life. Maybe you want to help a friend. Whatever the reason, this book is full of ways to use Nature to help explore how you feel.

If you are a professional working with children or you are a parent, this book provides a resource for you to use in whatever way you think best to support the children and young people in your care.

Whatever age we are, when loss happens, it's hard to manage. We may feel really upset, sad, angry, worried, anxious, scared, confused, guilty or just numb. One way of getting some balance back is to explore whatever we're feeling. We hope the activities in this book will help.

Contents

Imagine 7
Learning from Nature

The Medicine Wheel 10
What animals can teach us

Draw or Paint 13
Suggestions of drawing or painting things to do

Write 14
Suggestions of writing things to do

Memory and Loss Leaves 15
Leaves to cut out and draw or write on

Memory and Loss Tree 17
For sticking your leaves on

Big Leaves 18
Bigger leaves for a bigger tree

Changes 20
How change affects us

Lifetimes 24
Life cycles – long and short

Colouring 27
Pictures to colour in

Exploring the Feelings Tree 30
Finding out more

The Feelings Tree 31
Different feelings

Sticking Stickers 32
Things to do with stickers

Stickers 33
For sticking!

The Language of Flowers 34
Myths and meanings

Word Storms 40
A game to play

Snakes and Ladders of Loss 42
Another game

Feelings and Seasons 43
Thinking about feelings

Mandalas 44
What they are and how to use them

Labyrinths 49
What they are and how to walk them

Poems and Stuff 57
What other people have written

My Story 63
Sharing feelings

Information about Loss and Bereavement 69
What to expect

For Teachers 72
Information and suggested activities

Support Groups 78

beginning is an end is a

Imagine

You could either read this section yourself or ask someone to read it for you while you close your eyes and imagine...

Nature is all around us, but to really see it you have to get out in it. So let's take a walk through the seasons and you'll find that loss and change are all around.

Imagine it's winter. It's been raining for days. Maybe the rain has turned to sleet or snow. You pile on coats and boots and walk into the wind. There's not much colour about. The landscape is cold and bare; the earth is hard. It's a time when we may feel like staying indoors and going inward, hibernating like a bear or a tortoise. Just like in the days soon after someone has died or moved away, life is tough. But it won't always be so. Under the ground, things are happening. Trees and plants are saving energy for the new growth that will come.

Seeds beneath the earth are beginning to stir, reminding us that life goes on. More colourful times are on the way. Spring is coming.

Walking into spring, the sun begins to shine more often. Colour is returning to the world. The immediate shock and pain you may feel when someone dies or goes away doesn't last forever. Blossom covers the trees; bulbs burst out of the ground. Bright fresh green leaves appear – new life shows us that loss and death can be a beginning as well as an end.

And then it's summer. The days are bright; the sun stays longer. Parks and gardens fill with colourful flowers; imagine you can smell them. Did you know many of them are symbols of things, like roses for love and rosemary for remembrance? They remind us that even in very sad times there are happy moments, when life is for living and it's OK to laugh and have fun.

When Bonfire Night approaches and the days begin to shorten and the leaves change colour and start blowing off the trees, you know you're walking into autumn. Fruits and berries show us that the outside shape of things changes as time passes. A bud becomes a flower, a flower becomes a fruit and the fruit will eventually drop from the tree. But inside the fruit are the seeds from which new life will grow.

Life is always a journey full of change.

So we arrive back where we started. Autumn leads to winter, winter leads to spring, spring to summer, summer to autumn and autumn back to winter. Each season would not be possible without the one that came before it. They are all joined in one cycle of the seasons.

is part of life is part of death

Now let's take another walk…

back in time…

Imagine you are living hundreds of years ago. Our ancestors lived in a world which was much more in touch with the seasons and the wild animals that share our planet.

Imagine…there are no electric lights, no cars or buses, no planes, no big cities, no supermarkets, no cinemas, no television, no mobile phones, no play stations, no laptops. Imagine how dark the nights and how bright the stars are. Imagine it takes you days to walk to the nearest town; you have to grow your own food, make your own clothes, farm your own land. Horses are your new best friends!

Humans needed animals in ways we have long forgotten; animals have always had much to teach us. Have a look at the four animals of the Medicine Wheel in the next chapter.

The Medicine Wheel

Exploring the Medicine Wheel can help us to think about how we see things and what's happening to us...

The Medicine Wheel has been around for thousands of years. To our ancestors, 'medicine' was for getting back into balance with the cycle of the seasons. The wheel is used to help find balance at times when everything feels out of control. Experiencing a big loss in our lives is bound to knock us off balance. It's not easy to keep balance in our lives at the best of times. Not surprising, considering our bodies are made up of over 50 per cent water. Just try holding a bowl that's half full of water, swaying from side to side and trying to keep the water level!

The Medicine Wheel, or the Wheel of Life, is divided into four parts, one for each direction – north, south, east and west. It is really a Wheel of the Year, with an animal for each season. Each animal has a special quality – physical, emotional, mental and spiritual. Thinking about these different qualities can help us to begin to take care of those four aspects of ourselves and so begin to get our balance back.

Eagle is the animal of spring and helps us to focus on our spiritual needs. Eagle flies the highest and sees the biggest picture. When we suffer a big loss, we often want to hide away; we may not want to see people and it can be hard to concentrate. It's important to remember there's a big world out there full of places that it might feel exciting to go to, people it might feel good to spend time with, things it might feel fun to do. Thinking about Eagle flying high helps us to see our loss as part of a bigger picture.

Mouse is the animal of summer and helps us to focus on our emotional needs. Mouse's world is small. Mouse teaches us that solutions to problems might be right under our noses. Mouse has a gentle way of being in the world, using whiskers to sense what is around. Thinking about Mouse's whiskers helps us to focus on our senses, our emotions. Sometimes it's helpful to get in touch with and release powerful feelings, as long as we can find a safe way of doing so.

Bear is the animal of autumn and helps us to focus on our physical needs. Bear feeds up well before hibernating and then wakes in the spring, ready for action. When we have experienced a big loss, Bear teaches us to look after ourselves – to eat well and get lots of sleep and exercise. Bear also teaches us that it's OK to go inwards and think about what's happened when so much is going on and we may feel so out of control.

Buffalo is the animal of winter and helps us to focus on our mental needs. Buffalo is very wise and is the great provider. If Buffalo is going to be killed, his wish is that all parts of his body will be used – for food or for clothes or for tools. Buffalo reminds us to be resourceful and use all that we have; he shows us that everything has a purpose and a use. Sadness, for example, shows us how good happiness is.

The way to achieve balance and keep well is to take care of all four of these aspects of ourselves.

Make your own Medicine Wheel

Create a circle. How many different ways can you think of to do this?

- *Draw or paint one on a piece of paper.*
- *Create one on the floor with bits of material or paper.*
- *Make one outdoors with stones, bits of wood, sawdust or flour.*

Make an Animal Wheel. Draw, paint or find pictures of Eagle, Mouse, Bear and Buffalo, and decorate your wheel with them. Draw or write about the things you know or find out about each of these animals.

Make a Seasons Wheel. Draw or write about each season, or collect things to show what you like best about each season or what you like to do in each one.

Make a Four Directions Wheel. Mark North, South, East and West on your wheel. Draw or write about what these directions make you think of. See what you can find out about each direction online.

Sometimes drawing can help us explore what we're feeling...

Draw or Paint

...a tree or a bird or an insect or an animal you've seen

...the garden you'd like to have – its shape, its colours, the trees and plants and things you'd like to have in it

...your garden at home or a place in a park near you

...a flower and make up your own meaning for it (like the ones in the Language of Flowers chapter)

...a cycle of life

...something in your garden or in a park that makes you feel happy or sad

...the colours that each of the seasons make you think of (why do you think you chose those colours?)

Sometimes writing can help us to get feelings out from inside. Here are some suggestions you might try...

Write

- ...about an animal or an insect or a flower or a tree you've seen
- ...about a garden you'd like to have. What would you have in it? Would you grow vegetables?
- ...a story about a seed and what might happen to it
- ...about a plant or an animal you would like to be and why
- ...about a time when you felt happy or a time when you felt sad
- ...a poem about your garden or a park or an animal or an insect
- ...about which season feels the happiest to you and which feels the saddest and why

Memory and Loss Leaves

All of us find it hard to deal with losses in our lives. One reason is because whoever or whatever we've lost used to bring us happiness and now that's gone. Here's a way of exploring both sides of this coin...

You'll find some blank leaves and a Memory and Loss Tree on the next pages.

Choose a leaf:

- *Think of someone or something you've lost in your life.*
- *Draw or write your loss on the leaf.*

Choose another leaf:

- *Think of a happy memory you have.*
- *Draw or write your happy memory on the leaf.*

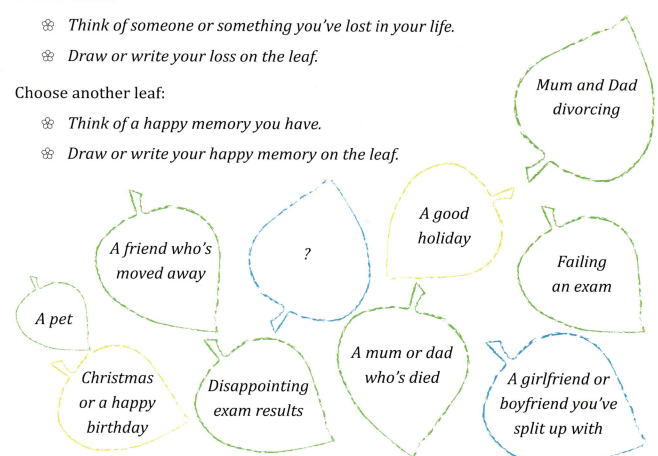

Cut out your leaves and stick them on the Memory and Loss Tree.

You could choose one colour for losses and another colour for happy memories. See if you can get an equal number of leaves of each colour on your tree.

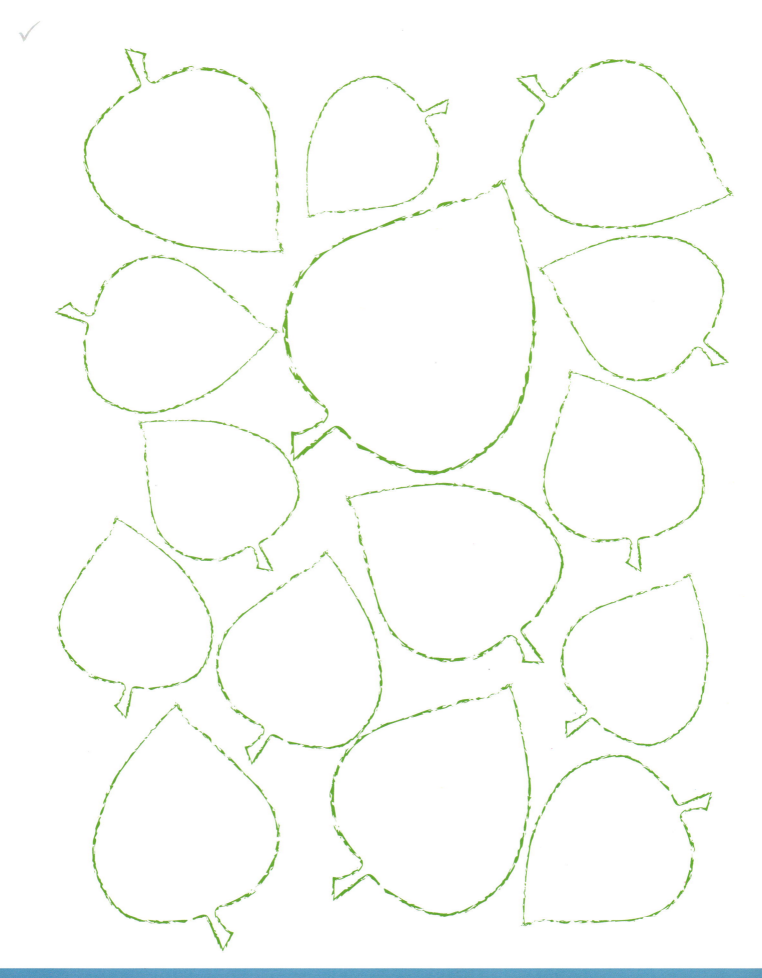

Memory and Loss Tree

*Here's a tree to stick your leaves on,
or you could make one of your own...*

Big Leaves

It's good to remember the person who is no longer in your life. A part of them will live on in your memory like flowers or trees that live on in their seeds or fruit. Here is another way of collecting memories and remembering…

- With friends or with your class, make a giant paper Memory and Loss Tree. Or see if you can find a broken or cut-off branch from a real tree to use.
- Here are some leaves that you can cut out for it.
- Or you could collect some real leaves and draw round them. Do you know what kinds of trees your leaves come from?
- Write on your leaves a memory or a loss or the name of a person or pet that's died or of someone who is no longer in your life.
- Sign your name if you'd like to, and then stick them on the tree.

Maple – Acer Pseudoplatanus

Changes

Life is full of changes; they happen all the time. Some changes are harder to cope with than others. Sometimes we know when change will happen; sometimes we don't. Sometimes we are ready for change; sometimes we're not. To change is to grow. This chapter helps us explore different types of changes and what happens before and after them…

Where do you think you would be on the Apple Tree circle?

Where do you think your mum or dad would be?

Where do you think your grandma or grandpa would be?

Make up your own Changes Circle, like the Apple Tree one. It could be about:

- *you*
- *an animal or insect you've seen*
- *your family.*

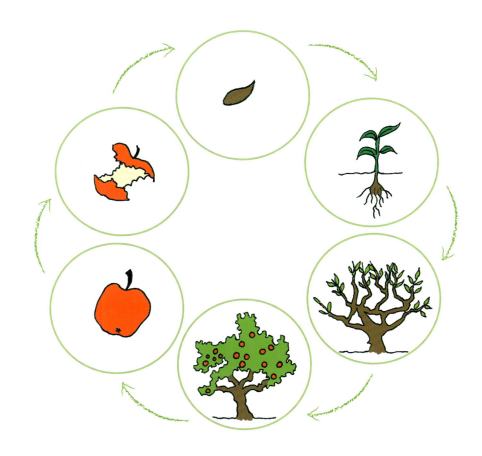

20

Exploring changes in a classroom or a group

Make a circle and pass an object round...

- *Say how it feels.*
- *Tell the story of where the object came from.*
- *Draw the object where it used to be.*
- *Say how it has changed over time.*
- *Discuss whether it will go on changing.*
- *Imagine what it might go on to be.*

Another word for change is...

- *Draw your own Change Line, like the Butterfly or Frog one.*
- *What does change make you feel like? Do you like change?*
- *In what ways have you changed in your life?*

The dictionary says metamorphosis means 'a complete change of physical form or appearance'. This happens to many living creatures. What creatures can you think of that go through metamorphosis?

If you visit a garden or a park or bit of woodland, you'll see that all of these places experience a sort of metamorphosis through the seasons every year. What signs can you find that this is happening? Is there moss or fungus growing where it wasn't last season? If there are some holly leaves, do the new and the old ones look the same? Are there berries where there used to be flowers?

Notice which plants die at the end of each year and which don't

Notice which things grow faster than others and which grow slower

Draw a picture each time you visit at different times of the year

Measuring changes in nature

Take a photo each time you visit at different times of the year and make a collage to show the changes

Keep a Changes Diary and write down the changes you notice each time you visit

Choose a special tree or plant and each time you visit measure its height or how big its trunk is or how much of the ground it covers

Memory making

Measuring changes = Making memories

If you have taken photos over a period of time, you will have created memories of how your garden or park or bit of woodland looked a few months earlier. If you have chosen a tree and measured how much it's grown, you will have created a memory of it when it was smaller.

Choose a garden light and hang it outside at home

Plant a bulb in a pot at home or in your classroom

Plant a tree or shrub in your garden

Choose a flower to plant in the Memory Meadow on the Seeds of Hope Children's Garden website

Memories are important, especially when someone dies or moves away. There are lots of ways to keep a memory alive. Here are some suggestions, and you'll find more in the Lifetimes chapter.

Lifetimes

All living things around us live for different lengths of time. We all find it hard when things don't work out as we expected them to, when lifetimes are cut short or when change happens when we don't expect it...

Nothing that is alive will live forever. Just as everything and everybody is born, so everything and everybody will die.

The length of a lifetime depends on who or what we're talking about and what happens during it. There are lots of different types of lifetimes in a garden or a park. Can you find out how long each of these lives?

Are these life cycles short or long? Does a birch tree live for the same length of time as an oak tree? Do all trees grow straight? If not, how could this affect the length of their lifetimes? Perhaps one creature's cycle of life is longer because another's is cut short. Lacewings and ladybirds will eat thousands of aphids every year. Birds will eat lacewings and snails. Foxes will eat birds.

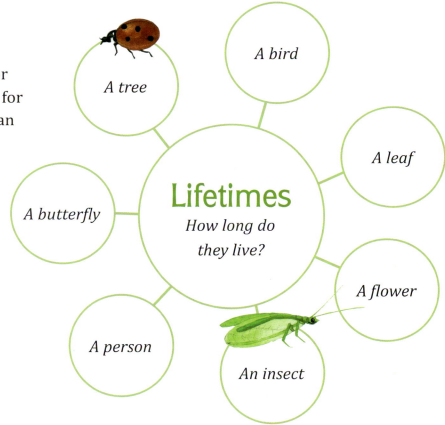

Lifetimes may be cut short for lots of reasons. A butterfly might break its wing, a person might become very sick, a tree might get blown over in a storm. Can you think of other things that could happen to change the length of a lifetime?

A lily of a day,
Is fairer far in May,
Although it fall and die that night;
It was the plant and flower of light.
In small proportions we just beauties see,
And in short measures, life may perfect be.

(from a poem by Ben Jonson)

Sometimes, the most beautiful things live for the shortest time – like cherry blossom. Can you think of other things that only live for a short time? Sometimes people are born with life-limiting conditions that mean they cannot live as long as others. When a lifetime has been cut short, we all have different ways of remembering. How do you remember?

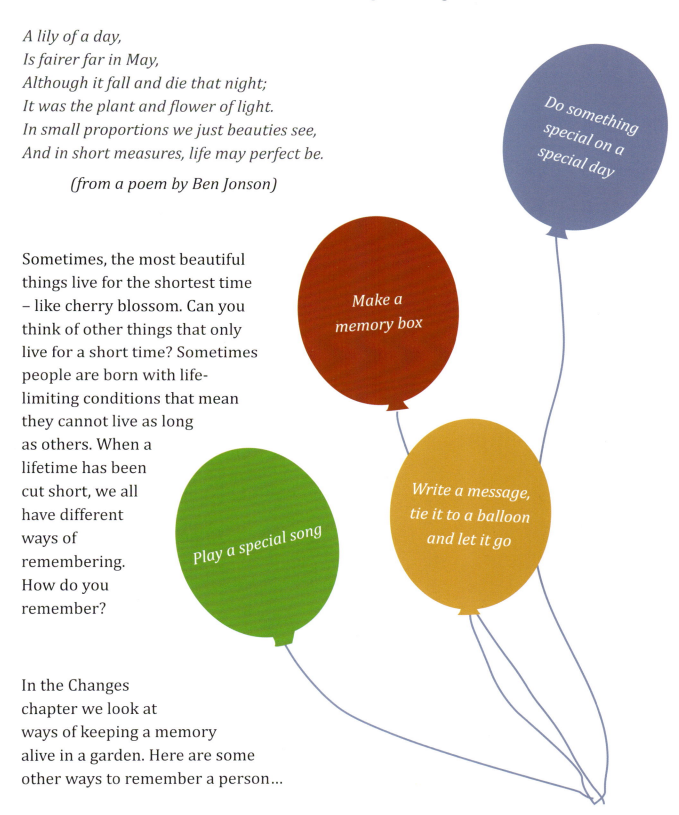

Do something special on a special day

Make a memory box

Write a message, tie it to a balloon and let it go

Play a special song

In the Changes chapter we look at ways of keeping a memory alive in a garden. Here are some other ways to remember a person…

Here's another way of exploring lifetimes.

Try making your own Life Line – all you need is paper and a pen. Choose whatever colours you like.

- *Draw a long horizontal line that runs the length of your paper – this represents the length of your life so far.*

- *Write the date you were born at the left-hand end.*

- *Think of all the important things that have happened to you in your life and mark them on your Life Line in the order in which they happened. The things that happened when you were young will go towards the left and the things that happened recently will go towards the right.*

- *Some things will be happy, some may be sad or scary. Put the happy things above your line and the sad or scary things below the line. Really, really happy things go high above the line and ordinary happy things go just above. Really, really sad things go way below the line and not so sad things go just below.*

- *If your piece of paper is big enough you could stick on some photos or drawings too.*

Colouring

Colouring can be fun. Even if you're feeling sad, it's ok to have fun. Colouring can also give you time to think and to work things out in your head. You can be as accurate as you like or go as mad as you like – there's no right or wrong!

- *Colour in these pictures using colours that are like the real ones or make up crazy colours – whatever you want!*
- *Can you spot any of these creatures in your garden or a park?*
- *Some of their Latin names are here – can you find the missing ones?*
- *Draw your own crazy caterpillar or butterfly and colour it in...*

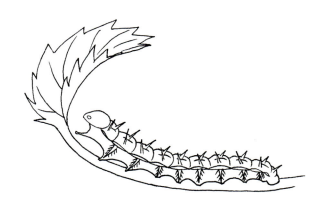

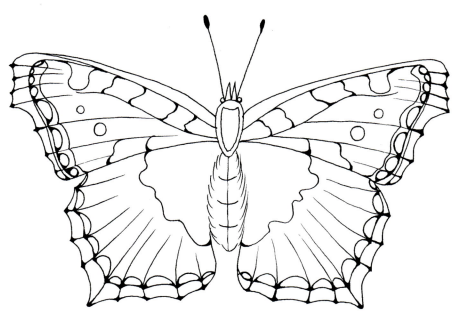

Small tortoiseshell – Aglais urticae

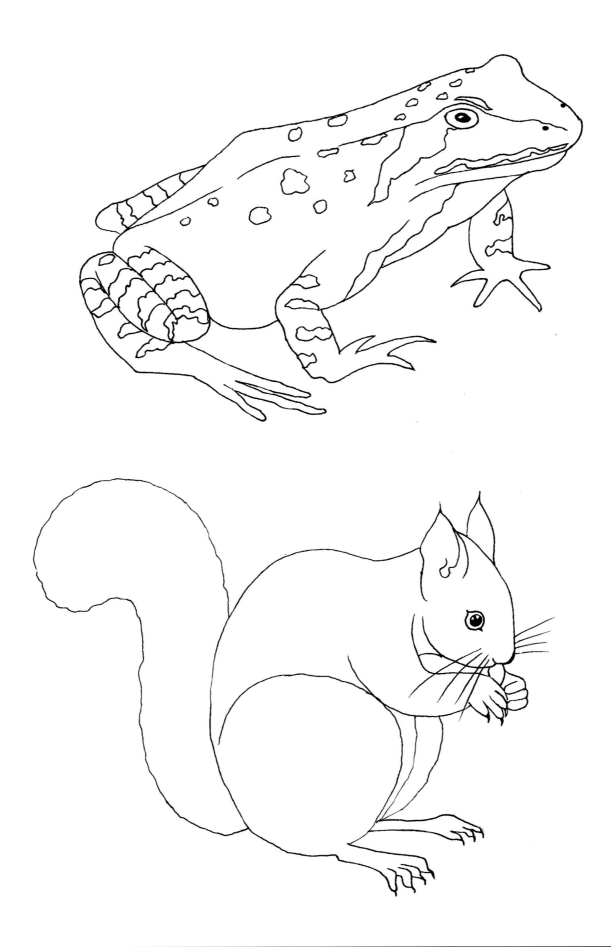

Exploring the Feelings Tree

Many of us find it hard to say what we're feeling. Sometimes it's easier to look at another person or creature and say whether we feel the same as they look.

- *Which bird looks happy?*
- *Which one looks sad?*
- *Which bird looks like it's struggling?*
- *Which one looks like you're feeling? Can you say why?*
- *Which bird would you not like to be?*
- *What do you think the three baby birds in the nest are feeling?*
- *Look at the bird lying on the ground. What do you think has happened?*
- *What do you think the bird with the flower is feeling?*
- *Look at the bird falling from the tree. What do you think it's feeling?*
- *Which bird would you like to have as a friend? Why?*
- *Which one would you try to stay away from?*
- *Which one looks kind?*
- *Which one looks unkind?*
- *Which ones look angry? Why do you think they might be angry?*
- *Which bird has the most friends? Why might that be?*
- *Which one looks lonely?*
- *If you were a bird, which one would you like to be?*
- *Choose some of the birds on the tree and make up a story about them – or write about all of them!*

The Feelings Tree

Sticking Stickers

Stickers can act as triggers for all sorts of things. Grab some glue and some scissors, cut out the stickers on the next page and see where they take you…

- Choose a sticker, stick it on a piece of paper and draw a picture around it
- Stick the dove sticker on a page and draw or write about where the dove is flying to or from
- Choose a sticker, stick it in the middle of the page and write any words it makes you think of around it
- Choose a sticker to decorate a picture you've already drawn
- Choose a sticker to go with a story you've written
- Make a pattern of stickers on a piece of paper like this 'S' shape
- Choose a sticker and write a story about it
- Choose a sticker and draw or write down the feeling it makes you think of
- Make up a sticker of your own

Stickers

The Language of Flowers

Some flowers are said to protect people from harm; some are said to heal. There are lots of stories, myths and legends attached to them. Here are just a few…

Did you know giving flowers is lucky? The ancient Egyptians thought so. Giving red flowers to someone who is ill is said to be lucky because they are the colour of blood and symbolise life. But beware! If flowers bloom out of season, taking them into a house or giving them to a friend is unlucky. Picking a flower from a grave and then throwing it away is also bad luck and it's said the place where the flower falls will be haunted!

Here are just a few meanings from the language of flowers. See if you can find some of these flowers and plants. Can you find meanings for other flowers? Or make up some of your own!

Spring flowers

Bluebell − constancy

In the Middle Ages, bowmen used bluebell sap to glue feathers onto arrows. It's said the bluebell keeps her head bowed because she's ashamed of her link to war and death. Do you know the rhyme 'In and out the dusky bluebells'? They are also known as Deadmen's Bells so be careful picking them in case you hear them ring!

Dandelion – Nature's oracle

Dandelion leaves have jagged tooth-like edges so in medieval times the dandelion was called 'dent-de-lion' – 'lion's teeth' in French. Some people believe the dandelion can tell the future, so it's known as Nature's oracle. It's said that the number of blows it takes to get rid of the seeds tells you what time is it, and the number of seeds left after you have blown on them once tells you how many years until your wedding day.

Forget-me-not – never forget me

A knight and his lady were walking along the banks of a river when the lady saw a pretty blue flower floating on the water; she was sad that it would be swept away. The knight leapt into the water to get it for her but was dragged down by the current. As he was drowning, he threw his lady the flower and cried, 'Forget me not!' For ever after the lady wound the flowers in her hair to remember him. It's said that if you plant forget-me-nots on the grave of someone you love, the plants will never die as long as you live. Forget-me-nots are unusual because you can see both blue and pink flowers on the same stem. Some people think that blue is for boys and pink is for girls. These little flowers symbolise the fact that, whoever you are, you will always be remembered.

Hawthorn – hope

Hawthorn is also called 'May' because it flowers in May. It symbolises hope because it signals the return of spring and summer. A wreath of May blossom crowns the Green Man, a pagan symbol for life. The maypoles that people used to dance around were made of hawthorn. It's sometimes called Fairy Thorn as it's believed to be haunted by fairies. In Devon it's thought unlucky to sit under hawthorn because the fairies might cast a spell on you! However, if you hang hawthorn outside a cowshed, the cows will give lots of milk.

Summer flowers

Daisy – feelings shared

Its old name was 'bruisewort' because it was supposed to heal bruises. The name daisy comes from the Old English name meaning 'day's eye' because a daisy opens its petals in the morning and closes them at night. It is believed that if you grab a whole bunch of daisies with your eyes shut and then count them, that will be the number of years till you get married. It's lucky to step on the first daisy of the year, and when you can put your foot over seven daisies at once it is said that summer has arrived!

Lavender – distrust

The name comes from the Latin word 'lavare', which means to wash. The Romans used lavender water to bathe in. Lavender can be burned to keep away witches and brides were told to bring it into the house to protect against cruelty. People believed that snakes would hide underneath the plant, which is why it symbolises distrust.

Rose – love

The Romans threw rose petals over their floors, their heroes, and even their wine. They also decorated tombs with roses as they believed this would protect them from evil spirits. The little god, Cupid, was given a rose by his mother, Venus, the Goddess of Love, and he gave it to the God of Silence. It was said that a rose carved into a ceiling meant that the conversation in the room should be secret (it should be 'sub rosa' – Latin for 'under the rose').

Rosemary – remembrance

The Latin name for rosemary, 'Rosmarinus', means 'dew of the sea' because it grew around the Mediterranean and was associated with Venus, the Goddess of love, who was supposed to have sprung from the sea foam. Because of this legend, rosemary became the symbol of faithfulness and was used at weddings and also at funerals, where it was thrown into coffins so the dead person would be remembered. Shakespeare wrote, 'There's rosemary, that's for remembrance.' One legend compares its growth to the height of Jesus, saying that after 33 years it grows broader, but never higher.

Autumn flowers

Blackberry – envy

Blackberries have become associated with the Devil in France and England. In France it's thought that the blackberry is black because the Devil spat on it. In England it's said that picking blackberries after Michaelmas Day (11 October) is bad luck because the Devil left a curse on them when he fell into some brambles and hurt himself. People used to believe that you could cure lots of illnesses by crawling through a bramble bush backwards (it's not true!).

Crab Apple – ill nature

The name 'crab' comes from an old Scandinavian word, 'skrab', meaning 'scrubby', which is what crab apple trees are like. If you peel an apple and throw the complete peel over your left shoulder, it is said that the letter it forms is the initial of your future husband or wife! When Shakespeare talked about 'roasting crabs', he didn't mean seaside ones, he meant crab apples.

'When roasted crabs hiss in the bowl, then nightly sings the staring owl.' (from 'Love's Labour's Lost' by William Shakespeare)

Crocus – cheerfulness

Crocuses used to be used to make saffron, which is how the town in Essex called Saffron Walden got its name. It took 4320 flowers to make one ounce of saffron so it was very expensive and only used by very rich people. The spring crocus is one of the first flowers to appear after winter, sometimes flowering in the snow. It is a symbol for being open to everything good that can come to us, which is how it got its meaning.

Sloe – difficulty

The sloe is the fruit of the blackthorn and it's said that Christ's crown of thorns was made from blackthorn. Perhaps this is why sloe is supposed to mean death and disaster if you bring it into the house. Folklore says that blackthorn blooms at midnight on Christmas Eve. In pagan times, branches of blackthorn were burned in fire festivals and the ashes scattered to make sure of a good harvest. Sloes are too bitter to eat but they make good wine and sloe gin.

Winter flowers

Ivy – friendship

The ancient Greeks gave newly-weds wreaths of ivy so they would stay faithful to each other. Bacchus, the God of Wine, wore an ivy wreath to stop himself getting a hang-over! Ivy growing up the walls of a house is said to protect it from evil. It was believed that drinking from a cup made of ivy wood would cure whooping cough and alcoholism!

Snowdrop – hope

Snowdrops are one of the first flowers to appear in the year and so they symbolise the hope of new life. They sometimes appear even before the snow has melted. Many people think they look like an angel on a snowflake. Medieval monks used them for healing wounds. Some say it is bad luck to pick them and bring them indoors. A single snowdrop in the house is seen as an omen of death because the petals look like a shroud.

Holly – am I forgotten?

Holly has always been said to protect against evil. A holly hedge around a field or house protects against bad luck. Its evergreen leaves and winter berries were linked with eternal life. Sometimes holly leaves are prickly up to about 3 metres high and then, where there is no need for protection, they become smooth. This is rather like in life when things are painful – if you keep on growing through the painful times, smoother times will be on the way.

Willow – sadness

In the fifth century BC, a Greek doctor, Hippocrates, wrote that chewing the bark of a willow tree could relieve pain and fever. (Maybe squirrels don't get headaches!) In 1829, a chemical called salicin was successfully isolated from willow bark and soon aspirin was developed from it. In the 20th century, over one trillion aspirin were swallowed throughout the world! Native Americans discovered that you can actually grow a whole new willow tree by taking a stem and sticking it in moist soil. The hormones in willows cause rapid root growth so they began to make their own 'willow water'. You could try it! Collect some willow twigs, remove the leaves, chop up the twigs and soak them in water overnight. Pour the willow water on your new plants and watch them grow!

Word Storms

Lots of us find it difficult to talk about death and feelings of loss and to find the right words. Here's an idea for a game that might help – suitable for ages 4 to 99!

Word Storms can be played in a car, in class, on a walk or up a tree! Everyone tries to think of as many other words as they can for the 'Word Storm' word. See how many you can get! You could search online for different words of use a dictionary or thesaurus.

Here are some examples in case you need them…

Word Storm: 'Dead'

❀ *Lost, gone to sleep, passed away, taken from us, at rest, at peace, in heaven, with God, in a better place, with the angels, snuffed it, kicked the bucket, six feet under, pushing up daisies, popped his clogs, brown bread (which is Cockney rhyming slang!).*

Word Storm: 'Different kinds of loss'

❀ *A favourite toy, a pet, a favourite game, a favourite piece of jewellery, falling out with a best friend, going to a different school to your friends, missing out on a holiday or a school trip, breaking up with a boyfriend or girlfriend, parents getting divorced, being fostered, being adopted, somebody dying, failing an exam, having your mobile stolen, moving house.*

Word Storm: 'Feelings'

❀ *Sad, happy, angry, pleased, scared, confident, numb, energetic, empty, excited, small, bouncy, unhappy, OK, alone, hopeful, warm, cold, high, low, smiley, depressed, quiet, noisy, tired, insecure, powerful, positive, frightened, jealous, popular.*

Word Storm cards

Try this game… You'll need some card and coloured pens.

❀ *Write your words onto pieces of card.*

❀ *Cut out and stick these faces onto other pieces of card.*

❀ *Sort out which word goes with which face.*

Snakes and Ladders of Loss

Sometimes, if we're sad, it helps to think about what makes us feel better as well as what doesn't. Grab a dice and have a go at the Snakes and Ladders of Loss! What would you put at the top of your snakes and bottom of your ladders?

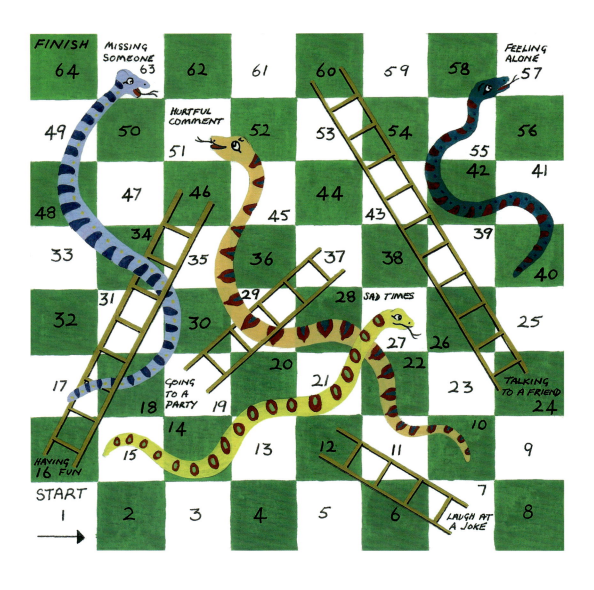

Feelings and Seasons

This is another way of exploring feelings. If sad things happen to us in one season, it may become a time of year when we always feel sad; if happy things happen in one season we may feel happy at that time of year. But all seasons are linked; one would not be possible without the other and one always leads to the next...

Have a look at the words in the circle.

- *Draw a line from each word to whichever season you think it fits into.*
- *Make up some of your own 'feelings' words and do the same for them.*
- *Pick a season and think of things that have happened to you in the months of that season. How do you feel about it?*
- *Which season are you looking forward to?*

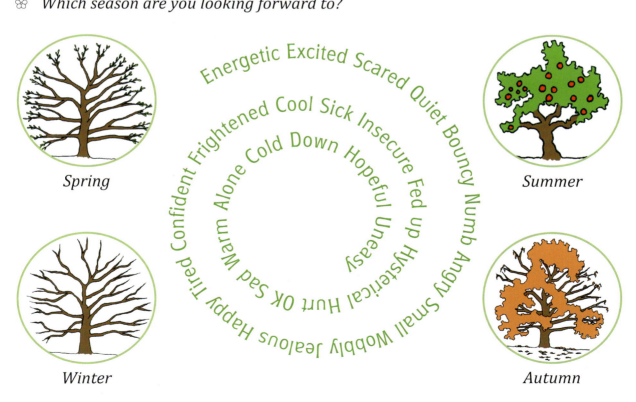

43

Mandalas

When we experience loss and we feel pain, it can be hard to face what we are feeling. If we keep our feelings inside us and suppress them, they can make life difficult for us in the future. Creating a mandala or colouring one in is a way of bringing these feelings out and looking at them. Looking into the centre of a mandala is a way of looking into the centre of ourselves. Have a go!

The 'circle with a centre' pattern is the basic structure of creation in the world as we know it. The planet Earth is part of a solar system, which is part of the Milky Way galaxy. Each is a mandala that is part of a larger mandala. It is a pattern seen in astronomy, biology, geology, chemistry, physics and all of Nature. Living things are made of cells and each cell has a nucleus; in all of them you will find circles with centres. The crystals that form ice, rocks and mountains are made of atoms. Each atom is a mandala.

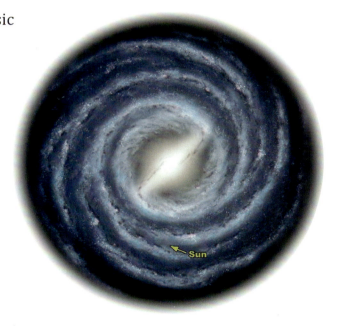

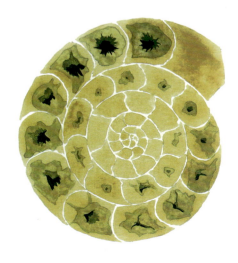

Gardens, parks and outside spaces are full of mandalas. See how many you can find. Have a look in flowers or at the rings found in tree trunks or the spiralling of a snail's shell. If you pick a toadstool and dry it out in an upright position over a piece of paper, it will release its spoors to form a mandala. Even the tiniest things, sometimes invisible, are all part of the circle of life.

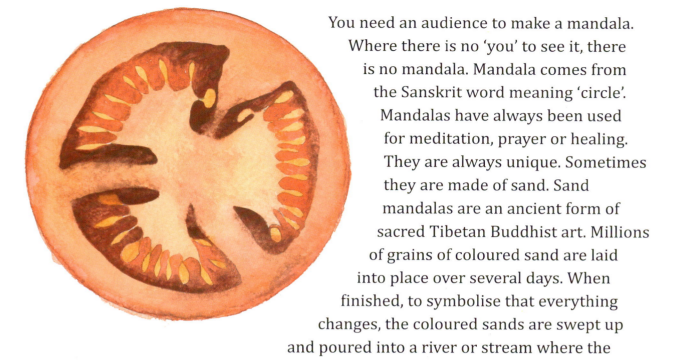

You need an audience to make a mandala. Where there is no 'you' to see it, there is no mandala. Mandala comes from the Sanskrit word meaning 'circle'. Mandalas have always been used for meditation, prayer or healing. They are always unique. Sometimes they are made of sand. Sand mandalas are an ancient form of sacred Tibetan Buddhist art. Millions of grains of coloured sand are laid into place over several days. When finished, to symbolise that everything changes, the coloured sands are swept up and poured into a river or stream where the waters carry the healing energies throughout the world.

See what you can find out about mandalas – where's the biggest one? Who created mandalas in the 12th century? Where might you find sand mandalas? There are some types of mandala that you can walk through. These are called labyrinths. Have a look at the Labyrinth chapter to find out more about them.

All sorts of people use mandalas in all sorts of situations, often to help them cope when life is hard.

Create your own mandala

❀ *Draw a mandala based on something you've seen in a garden or a park.*

❀ *Make up your own mandala and colour it. When you do this, it is said that you become part of the circle...the circle of life.*

Create a Mandala Labyrinth

❀ *Get together with a group of friends, or your class at school, and each draw a mandala. Or, if you're doing this on your own, draw lots of mandalas! Hole-punch and, if you can, laminate everyone's mandalas. Join them together with string to create a mandala chain.*

❀ *Tape some strips of lining paper together to make a giant sheet and then draw a labyrinth pattern on it to create a path (see how to do this in the Labyrinth chapter).*

❀ *Or mark out a labyrinth pattern on the ground with some thick string or rope. Lay your mandala chain along the path to form your Mandala Labyrinth.*

❀ *Walk it!*

A mandala to colour in

The beautiful stained glass rose windows found in many cathedrals and churches are based on mandalas.

Here's how to create your own stained glass window pattern... Starting at the top dot (Fig 2), connect every fifth point round the circle to create a dodecagram or 12-pointed star, like this (Fig 3)...

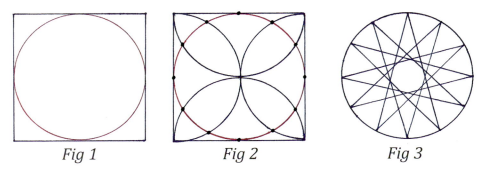

Fig 1 *Fig 2* *Fig 3*

Draw 12 small circles within the rays of the star (Fig 4). Find the outer point of these circles and connect every fifth one as before to create a smaller dodecagram star (Fig 5). Connect every fourth point of the large dodecagram star to form an equilateral triangle. Draw a circle within that triangle (Fig 6) and that will show you the window's size.

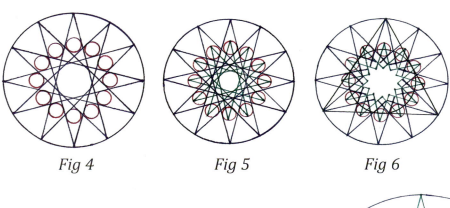

Fig 4 *Fig 5* *Fig 6*

And you've made your very own pattern for the rose window in Chartres Cathedral!

Labyrinths

Exploring labyrinths by walking their path can help us to find ways to go forward following a loss...

A labyrinth is an ancient symbol for the journey of life. It is a sacred space that combines the imagery of the circle and the spiral in one path. We can walk the path just as we walk life's journey. The path is never straight, and we may not be sure which way it will take us but, if we keep going, we can be sure that we will arrive in the centre. There is only one starting point (like birth) and only one end (like death) and in between is like living.

So are labyrinths and mazes the same?

❀ *Try these mazes...*

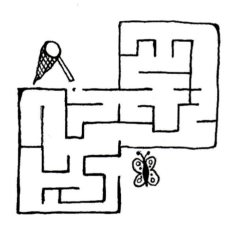

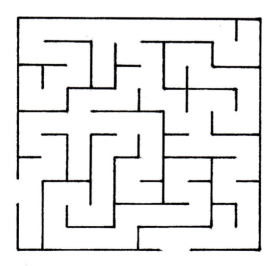

❀ *Now try this labyrinth...*

❀ *What differences did you find?*

Labyrinths have been around a long time…

In Greek mythology, King Minos of Crete had a labyrinth built in which to hide the Minotaur, a terrible monster that was half man and half bull. The hero, Theseus, killed the Minotaur. He was helped by the beautiful princess, Ariadne, who gave him a ball of string. He tied one end to the entrance of the labyrinth and then used the trail of string to find his way back out of the labyrinth. Actually, as you'll find if you try tracing the labyrinth path above, he wouldn't have needed it!

Since then, the ancient pattern of the labyrinth has been found in many sacred cultures around the world. See what you can find out about how the Hopi tribe in America or the Aborigines in Australia used labyrinths. Labyrinth designs have been used on pottery, tablets and tiles dating as far back as 4000 years.

All sorts of spiritual groups use labyrinths; religious groups use them as a way of exploring the journey of faith that leads to their 'god'. To draw a labyrinth, you start with a cross – as you'll see at the end of this chapter. The cross is one of the most ancient human symbols and is used by many Christian religions all over the world. Labyrinth designs can be found in many churches in Europe. One of the most famous is in Chartres Cathedral in France, which was built in 1200 AD. It used to be walked – often on the knees! – in place of an actual pilgrimage to Jerusalem.

The Chartres labyrinth looks like this…

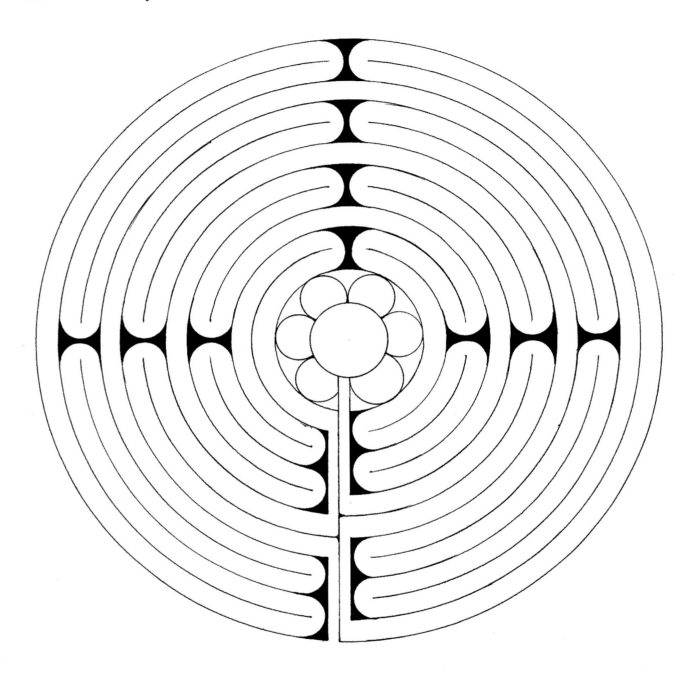

Try following the path with a pen…

Did you notice that the path takes you to and fro between the four quarters of the labyrinth? They represent the physical, emotional, spiritual and mental parts of us. Loss affects us all in all four ways. We keep our balance by keeping these four aspects of ourselves in balance. Do you remember the Medicine Wheel in the second chapter?

Labyrinths are giant walking mandalas – like the
ones in the Mandala chapter. Mandalas and labyrinths
are archetypal collective symbols that transcend
all cultures and religions. Walking a labyrinth is like
doing a mini-pilgrimage into yourself, an invitation to
think about who you are and what's happened to
you in life. When you walk a labyrinth, you give
it power and meaning. The more a labyrinth
is walked, the more powerful it becomes.

Try making one...

and walking it...

See what happens!

Ways to walk a labyrinth

There is no right way to walk a labyrinth… You could try one of these or make up your own.

For these first three walks you will need to choose something to put in the centre of the labyrinth – a bowl or basket or a bag or box…

The 'Goodbye' Walk

Think of someone or something that you've lost in your life. It might be a person or a pet who has died, or someone who has moved away or a favourite toy you have lost. Write a message to them or just write down their name if you like. Walk the path with your message, place it in the centre and walk out. When everyone has placed their messages, decide together what you would like to do with them to let your message go.

The 'Memory' Walk

Design your own labyrinth in memory of someone and place landmarks of special things along the way, or draw a finger labyrinth at home and draw your special landmarks on that. As you do the Memory Walk, stop at each landmark and take time to feel what it means to you. Imagine if you could see the person once more for five minutes. What would you like to say to them? Write this down and place it in the centre of the labyrinth when you arrive there. Before you leave, decide how you would like to let your message go.

The 'Letting Go' Walk

Find a stone or leaf and imagine putting into it all your problems, feelings, and thoughts that are not helpful to have at the moment. Hold the stone or leaf in your hand and concentrate on it as you walk the labyrinth. When you get to the centre, leave it there and walk out. Before you leave, decide what you would like to do with your stone or leaf to let all those feelings and thoughts go.

The 'Whatever' Walk

Walk, hop, skip, jump…follow the path in whatever way you feel like! Fast or slow, forwards or backwards. If you're with your class, some people could stand round the outside of the labyrinth and clap hands to a rhythm or play musical instruments or blow bubbles. When you finish your walk, swap places with one of the people round the outside till everyone has done the walk.

The 'Score a Goal' Walk

The middle of the labyrinth is the goal. You choose what the goal is. It might be helping someone once a day or scoring a goal in your next football match or passing a test or exam or walking a dog or it might be a secret goal. If you are with a class, you might decide on one goal for everyone. Then everyone walks the labyrinth thinking of their goal.

The 'Animal' Walk

Choose an animal or bird or insect and walk the labyrinth as if you were this creature. If you want, make the noises they would make.

Looking at labyrinths

- *Can you think of any ways in which walking a labyrinth is like journeying through life?*

- *Try writing a poem about the labyrinth.*

- *Search online for all the places in the world where there are labyrinths. Plot them on a map of the world. Find out what was happening to the people who built them and what life was like in their societies.*

- *Find as many different labyrinth patterns as you can. They may link up with the mandalas in the Mandala chapter – take a look!*

- *Make your own labyrinth using coloured wool or string or flour or sand, or draw one by starting with a cross, like this...*

Maybe the way we draw a labyrinth – starting from the inside and working outwards – has something to tell us about how we might live our lives... Maybe what's on the inside is more important than what's on the outside.

Poems and Stuff

Lots of people have written stories and poems about loss and death, about times they felt happy or sad. Sometimes reading what other people have written can give us ideas for what we'd like to write…

The Little Ship
Anon

I stood watching as the little ship sailed out to sea. The setting sun tinted her white sails with a golden light…and as she disappeared from sight a voice at my side whispered, 'She is gone.'

But the sea was a narrow one. On the farther shore a little band of friends had gathered to watch and wait in happy expectation. Suddenly they caught sight of the tiny sail and, at the very moment when my companion had whispered, 'She is gone', a glad shout went up in joyous welcome, 'Here she comes.'

Life and death are one

Kahlil Gibran

For life and death are one, even as the river and the sea are one.
In the depth of your hopes and desires lies your silent knowledge of the beyond;
And like seeds dreaming beneath the snow your heart dreams of spring.
Trust the dreams, for in them is hidden the gate to eternity...

'More things grow in the garden than the gardener sows.'
Spanish proverb

Arnie the Acorn

Caroline Jay

Arnie the acorn lived on the end of a branch of a huge oak tree. He lived high up above the ground but Arnie didn't know this because he couldn't see the view. All he could see were lots of leaves and his friends, the other acorns. They all started off small and bright green like him and over the days they grew bigger and bigger. They had lots of visitors. Two ravens made a giant nest just above Arnie's head. They flew in and out for days with sticks and moss and bits of bright shiny wire. Then the mother raven sat on the nest and soon Arnie heard sounds he hadn't heard before, the cheeping of chicks. Furry caterpillars visited Arnie's branch. They crawled out onto the leaves and began eating them. Arnie had never seen anything eat so much so fast. Whole leaves disappeared in minutes! Sometimes squirrels would race past chasing each other. Sometimes one of them would stop and look at Arnie and then move on.

'What does she want?' Arnie wondered.

The hot sun grew cooler and the days got shorter and more windy. Arnie noticed that the leaves around him were turning yellow and his friends, the other acorns, were turning brown. One day a very scary thing happened. His best friend, the acorn nearest to him, suddenly fell out of the tree. Arnie was looking at him when he slipped out of the cup he had always sat in and disappeared, down, down and out of sight. Over the next few days, Arnie noticed more of his friends disappearing. It made him sad. Then one day Arnie felt himself slipping. He tried his best to hang on but he couldn't stop himself falling, falling, falling.

'Help!' he shouted.

Down past the brown leaves, past branches he had never seen before, down, down, down he fell. Just when he thought there couldn't be any more down to go, he landed with a bump and a bounce on the ground.

'Where am I?' he asked, dazed.

'You're on the ground, stupid!' said a passing woodlouse who was busy eating bits of old wood that had fallen from the oak tree.

Before Arnie had time to ask any more questions, two small claws whisked him up off the ground. A squirrel was racing away with him towards a clearing in the wood. She dropped Arnie and started digging furiously. Quick as a flash, Arnie felt himself being tumbled into a hole and everything went black.

'Help!' shouted Arnie for the second time that day.

Arnie didn't know how long he stayed in the dark. He wasn't scared. It felt warm and safe where he was although he missed his friends and all the creatures that used to visit. His happy memories of them cheered him up though and he was pleased that he'd always have his memories.

One day, a most surprising thing happened. Arnie began to feel the warmth of the sun above him and it made him want to push upwards so he did and all of a sudden he burst out of the ground into the light! He could feel the sunshine again like when he was an acorn only now he realised he wasn't an acorn any longer. He had long roots that went down into the earth and made him feel strong and a long stem that went up into the air. More amazing than that, he had leaves!

'How cool is this!' thought Arnie.

The days passed and Arnie grew and grew. He saw things he'd never seen before. He saw the ground stretching away in all directions covered in small creeping creatures. He saw birds of all shapes and sizes, many of them much smaller than the ravens he remembered. He grew more and more branches, his stem began to look like a tree trunk. He grew hundreds of leaves and stretched them out into the warm air.

Every so often whilst all this growing was going on, Arnie had to rest. The days would grow shorter, the sun shone less and the air grew colder. When this happened, all Arnie's leaves fell off and he went very quiet and still. Sometimes snow would cover his bare branches.

Then, many weeks later, when the warm rains came and the sun shone once more , he grew all his leaves back again. He felt caterpillars tickling and birds nesting and insects crawling and squirrels racing along his branches. He saw beautiful butterflies fluttering above his highest leaves. The best thing was the day he discovered that he had grown acorns of his own! And all the time that all of this was happening, Arnie was watching the world.

'Wow!' he said. 'How amazing that all this was always here but I just couldn't see it before!'

'To everything there is a season
and a time for every purpose under heaven,
a time to weep and a time to laugh,
a time to mourn and a time to dance.'
Ecclesiastes 3: 1, 7, 8

'He who plants a garden plants happiness.'
Chinese proverb

Kind hearts are the gardens

Henry Wadsworth Longfellow

*Kind hearts are the gardens,
Kind thoughts are the roots,
Kind words are the flowers,
Kind deeds are the fruits.
Take care of your garden
And keep out the weeds.
Fill it with sunshine,
Kind words and kind deeds.*

'A garden is a friend you can visit anytime.'
Unknown

'Bread feeds the body, indeed,
but flowers feed also the soul.'
The Koran

She dwelt among the untrodden ways

*William Wordsworth
(on the death of his baby daughter Lucy)*

*She dwelt among the untrodden ways
Beside the springs of Dove,
A maid whom there were none to praise
And very few to love;*

*A violet by a mossy stone
Half hidden from the eye!
Fair as a star, when only one
Is shining in the sky.*

She lived unknown, and few could know
When Lucy ceased to be;
But she is in her grave, and oh,
The difference to me!

'For every flower that opens in your garden,
another wound is healed in your heart.'

Unknown

Do not stand at my grave and weep

Mary E. Frye

Do not stand at my grave and weep
I am not there. I do not sleep.
I am a thousand winds that blow.
I am the diamond glints on snow.
I am the sun on ripened grain,
I am the gentle autumn rain.
When you awaken in the morning's hush,
I am the swift uplifting rush
Of quiet birds in circled flight.
I am the soft stars that shine at night.
Do not stand at my grave and cry,
I am not there: I did not die.

'In mind a constant thought,
in heart a silent sorrow!'

Anon

We will remember them

Laurence Binyon

They shall grow not old, as we that are left grow old;
Age shall not weary them, nor the years condemn.
At the going down of the sun and in the morning,
We will remember them.

My Story

These young people have been kind enough to share their stories with us. Sometimes reading about what others have been through and how they kept going can make us feel less alone. Sometimes it can give us ideas for something we'd like to write...

Lewie Jones
by his big sister Charlie

My first memory of Lewie is at the hospital the day after he was born. He was really small, swamped by a mountain of blanket. When Mum said Charlie do you want to hold him I almost said NO. He looked too small and fragile to hold, my hands suddenly felt like big planks of wood.

Soon I was able to bath him, change his nappy, feed him, put him to bed, take him on walks, push him in the swing. Lewie blue shoes he became because of the colour of his shoes. And on birthdays (with the help of Mum) we would receive a birthday card from him with a blue footprint.

'Where's ma boy?' Dad would say as he came in from work and out Lewie would run into Dad's arms. 'My Daddy!' Lewie would shriek, but soon he would be off playing in the garden with his ca-cars.

Saturday 30th of July 2005. Mum decides we need to go out.

'Charlie can you get Lewie in the car?'

As I got Lewie in the car a feather flew down and landed on his nose. I tickled him and told him to blow, but he didn't understand and licked it instead. I laughed and just brushed it away. When we returned home from shopping, I got Lewie out his car seat the same feather was caught on Lewie's T-shirt. Oh look Lewie it's back.

That evening Lewie was really moany and restless, Mum was cooking so I put him in his highchair but he screamed 'Out!' and started retching. Mum grabbed him and stripped him down to his vest, he was really sweating.

'Is it a fish bone?' Dad said

'I don't know!' Mum shouted

'Just call an ambulance!'

'There's no time, we'll drive ourselves!'

Mum held Lewie, he kept retching and his eyes started rolling in his head. It was very scary but also very exciting. We got to the hospital and the lady rushed us straight through. They wired him up to this machine to check his oxygen. They needed him to eat to see if anything was stuck in his throat but he wouldn't, he just wanted to sleep.

Me and Imo were starving so Dad took us home. At about half nine Mum called Dad to say she had to stay the night and could he bring some spare clothes. Imo wanted to go with Dad but I said I would be all right at home. You have no idea how much I regret not going back, to see him one last time. I just stayed at home and watched TV...typical teenager, too lazy to get up. I will never forget that.

The next day at 2 o'clock Aunty Lisa came and told me and Imogen to come with her to the hospital. She had been crying. I kept thinking I know Lewie is poorly but you don't need to cry he is coming home soon, then I thought maybe he has died then I told myself off for being so stupid. We arrived at the hospital and Imogen noticed Thomas the Tank Engine stickers on the wall.

'I'm glad Lewie is in this bit, he will like these.'

Lisa didn't answer. Then I felt crushed. I didn't want to go any further. I knew it I could feel he had died. Just by looking at my Auntie's face I could tell. Imogen's little voice seemed distant and it didn't feel like me walking, I looked at Imogen and I knew what was about to happen and I felt so guilty, like it was my fault, she still had no idea what was about to happen.

We got to some big double doors and walked straight through, but a nurse stopped me.

'I'll bring your Mum and Dad out.'

'No!' I screamed and I felt myself push past her, I hated her. I felt like saying how dare you. I completely forgot about Imogen, I knew she was still holding my hand. Mum and Dad came to the door, I knew Mum had been crying, but I had never seen my Dad cry before, it was a shock. I looked into my Dad's eyes and he looked away.

'What!' nobody answered.

'What's happened?' I shouted. 'What's wrong?'

'He's gone,' Mum said.

'You're joking!' I screamed. 'Stop it now, you're joking. No!'

'Do you want to hold him?' Mum asked.

I snatched his body out of her arms and stupidly thought it would be like a fairy tale and if my tears fell on his cheek he would wake up. I sang Barney and Thomas the Tank Engine and the Wiggles over and over in my head hoping he would hear.

Finally we had to leave. Saying goodbye was the hardest thing that I have ever had to do. We left Lewie with Dog Dog his favourite soft toy. We got in the car. I sat next to his empty car seat, his juice bottle and coat. As I got out the car I noticed something white on the floor, Yes it was the feather, our feather. I still have it. I always will!

Afterwards

Some days I'm fine, other days I hope that when I close my eyes and go to sleep I don't wake up. I hate the way that I will be watching TV and then a little boy will come on screen and my whole body tenses.

I find myself not saying things to my family because it might make them sad. It is awful watching a man cry but in a way it is worse watching him trying to hide it. Sometimes all you need is a hug but other times it's nice to be left alone. Death is not an embarrassing thing. Do not be afraid to mention someone's lost one. It is not possible for you to upset them any more than they already are. If they do not want to talk then they will tell you. I have found round school people who once talked to me now avoid me. People need to learn to ask questions, I love talking about Lewie. Again everyone is different.

Lewie died at 19 months old of Hypertrophic Cardiomyopathy, an undiagnosed heart condition that shows no symptoms – our lives have been changed forever.

I am sad because I lost my remote control car.

Ariful

I don't like heaven because my cat and fish didn't come back from there.

Felix

I hate the builders. They took my ball. I felt sad, cross and furious. I said 'I hate you.' It was my favourite ball. I couldn't play with my granddad anymore. I liked my ball best of all.

Ryan

I lost my dog. I dropped my dog on the road. I felt worried because I did not know where it was. I found it. I was happy.

Jericho

After my mother died

by Richard Penn

My family consists of me, my brother Josh (9), my Dad and my Mum, who tragically died of a sudden asthma attack on the 7th November 2004 when I was 12 and my brother just 7.

It was only after that day that I understood the meaning of the phrase, 'You never truly appreciate something until it is gone.' It was then that it dawned on me the full scale of work and time my mother had put into our family and community around us, whether it be being PTA Chairman or decorating the new bathroom. After she died, our whole lifestyle collapsed around us. You don't just worry about the fact that you'll never see the individual again, you also have to try and contemplate the prospect of the future, and how your life has been turned upside-down with your normal daily routine from waking up, to going to bed being all altered.

When I lay in bed in the following weeks after my mother's death, I lay there worrying anxiously about what was to come. Who was to look after Josh and I when my Dad was still at work? How could my brother and I produce an evening meal every day that was substantial enough to live off?

However, now we have adapted and changed. We have a daily routine that works. The difficulties nowadays are minor and are to do with, say, picking me up or my brother up from school when we have a rugby match. So I have to miss my normal bus and find someone to look after my brother during the school holidays when our child minder is away. But now I am getting the age where I can look after Josh and take more responsibility for myself.

Over time what I think is improving is our realisation of Mum's death and our adaptation to living with its problems. For example now I don't really worry about the future any more than anyone else. And her death does not affect my lifestyle nearly as much as when she first passed away.

My granddad died. All I had left was his diary. I felt sad.

Lauren

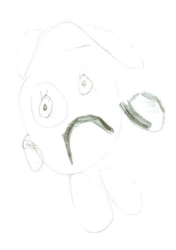

I lost my teddy. My brother lost it where I couldn't find it. When I hunted with my brother I couldn't find it. I felt sad every single day. I really missed my teddy.

Sian

My brother Jamie died. I was sad. My sister wasn't born then. I really loved Jamie. I'm sad Jamie's in heaven.

Luke

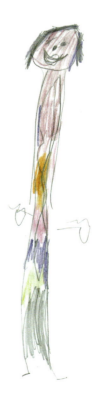

I lost my mum. I felt scared. I thought I wouldn't see her again. I found my mum at Argos. I felt happy.

Lucy

Information about Loss and Bereavement

- It is helpful to give children truthful, clear answers to their questions.

- They need loving and supportive acceptance of whatever their reactions might be.

- They need opportunities to talk about how they're feeling if they want to and also to know that it's OK not to talk.

- They need their familiar daily routines to continue as much as is possible.

- It is helpful to talk about the person who has died or gone away and to share how you are feeling about the situation – children learn about grief from watching the adults around them.

- If someone has died, it is much more helpful to use the words 'died' and 'dead' than euphemisms like 'gone to sleep' or 'gone away' or 'lost'.

- Children in general are unable to stay with their grief for any length of time; it is quite normal for them to dip in and out of it like jumping in and out of a puddle. They may be sad one minute and off out to play the next – this in no way negates the fact that they are sad and upset.

- Special occasions like birthdays, anniversaries, Christmas, Mother's Day and Father's Day may be especially difficult; an acknowledgement of this can help.

- At school, if curriculum activities centre around one of these days or around death or loss, it's helpful to discuss this in advance and give choices and alternatives when possible.

- At school, the provision of somewhere quiet to go if things get too much can be helpful.

- At school, bereaved children may find it hard to concentrate so need to be shown understanding; however, they also need to be treated the same as everyone else as far as possible.

Some thoughts on children's understanding of death and their possible reactions…

All children and young people, like adults, will react in different ways.

Under 5 years

Children under 5 years old cannot understand that death is final and irreversible so will ask the same questions over and over again and keep expecting the person who has died to reappear. They have difficulty understanding the concept of 'forever'. They may be concerned about the physical well-being of the dead person. They think in very concrete terms and can easily be confused by euphemisms. They can think of time as moving in a circle. Their daily routines are made up of repeated events; so with death, children think we live, we die, we live again. Their thinking can also be magical; if they can have imaginary friends who come and go, then so can the dead person. They sometimes work through their grief through play – games involving 'dead dollies' are perfectly normal. They are likely to be clingy and anxious and may revert to more babyish behaviour. They become very sensitive to loss or separation, so routine and reassurance are very important.

5–11 years

Children gradually begin to understand that death is irreversible and will happen to everyone, but they still resist the idea that it will happen to them (or in some cases become obsessed that it might). This denial may lead them to act as if nothing has happened. On the other hand, they may become obsessed by the subject of death and be unable to think about anything else. They may feel guilty and need reassurance that their behaviour did nothing to cause the death. Feelings may run deep and children may need help to bring them to the surface; looking at photos together, talking about memories and talking to friends and teachers can help. They begin to get a sense of the injustice of things. They begin to see themselves less as the centre of the universe and begin to understand others' feelings more; they may try to 'protect' family members from further pain by keeping their feelings to themselves. Or there may be other reasons for keeping feelings secret; they may feel bad about a feeling. For instance, if the death has been inevitable, they may feel a sense of relief that they can now get on with their lives. Children react in countless different ways. They can only tolerate grief in small doses and will then need to change the subject, to escape, to go and play.

Teenagers

Teenagers' feelings of grief are complicated by their attempts to become independent adults whilst needing the support they received as children. They too may feel guilty, as if they are in some way responsible for the death. If a parent has died, they may try to take on their responsibilities. Their understanding that death is universal and inevitable means it's also personal and teenagers may need to keep this thought at a distance. They may feel very fearful. They may find it easier to confide in friends rather than family members.

Signs of grief

These are some of the more common signs of grief in children and young people: crying, disturbed sleep patterns, nightmares, bed wetting, attention seeking, becoming more aggressive, more clingy, worried, fearful of change, sick, having difficulty concentrating, having relationship problems, eating problems, having suicidal thoughts. In most cases, with love, support and continued routines, these symptoms will pass. However, they should become a cause for concern if a child becomes withdrawn and ceases to be able to function on a daily basis. Specialised help should then be sought.

For Teachers

You are the person with whom children spend most of their time during school terms. You are therefore uniquely placed to help and support a child who is bereaved or suffering loss of any kind. None of us, old or young, can escape loss; the question is how it is managed. When handled well, many future problems in life can be avoided. The work you do with children in this difficult area will have far-reaching value in their lives.

The best way to support a bereaved child is to understand how you yourself feel about loss and death so that you can be as comfortable as possible when talking to the child about it. A helpful way to do this is to look at a loss in your life – it doesn't have to be a death. How did you feel? What did you need? What was helpful? Generally the answers will be similar for children.

It's important to do some preparation before talking to a bereaved child. Take into account what is known about the child's situation. What culture have they grown up in? Who are the significant adults in their lives? The effect of the death on the child will always be dependent upon the nature of the relationship that child had with the person who's died. How emotionally and physically close were they? How traumatic was the death? Did the child see it? Did they hear anything? What have they been told? What support is already in place?

General suggestions at school

- Wherever possible, treat death as a natural extension of what is already being taught.

- Include this teaching over time as children's understanding of death changes as they grow older.

- When teaching about death, perhaps include an activity to identify what beliefs each child holds and what they have been taught at home.

- If you are planning a school trip where issues around death and dying may come up and you have a bereaved child in your class, explain what is going to happen and give them a chance to opt out. Alternatively, you might consider asking them if they'd like to talk to you on their own.

- Consider any 'Ground Rules' you might want to set for children (e.g. listen to each other; help each other; no question is stupid – if you don't have the answer you will find someone who does).

- Wait for any personal stories of loss to be offered rather than asking for them.

- Reassure that tears are OK.

- Arrange for support to be available – ensure the children know exactly who they can talk to and when.

- Encourage honest expression of feelings, whether negative or positive (see the Memory and Loss Tree chapter).

- Allow for ongoing processing – some children may not be able to express their feelings at the time.

- Consider making a giant Memory and Loss Tree with the whole class and invite children to add Memory and Loss Leaves over the following weeks.

- Consider using circle time or thoughtful time to allow for any thoughts that might arise.

A summary of activities in the book

We hope these activities will be useful in the delivery of PSHE Education.

- An imaginative journey through the seasons and the cycle of life.

- The Medicine Wheel information and activities.

- Suggestions of things to draw, paint or write about.

- A Memory and Loss activity using leaves and a tree – a giant communal activity for the whole class.

- A Changes activity to encourage discussion about the changes that occur in life.

- A Lifetimes activity to explore the different nature of lifetimes.

- Pictures to colour in.

- A Feelings Tree – a visual activity to explore feelings.

- Stickers and suggestions of ways in which to use them.

- A Language of Flowers section with information on the meanings of flowers and associated myths and legends – to promote creative writing or for use in project-based work.

- Word Storms and Snakes and Ladders of Loss – games for all ages.

- A Feelings and Seasons activity – a word-based activity to explore feelings.

- Mandala information and activities.

- Labyrinth information and activities.

- Examples of poems and stories to offer springboards for discussion and/ or creative writing.

- Some personal accounts from bereaved children to promote understanding, awareness and shared experience.

- Some general information about common aspects of behaviour in bereaved children of different ages.

Suggestions for a primary school activity

Intentions

- to help children explore loss and change
- to help children better understand the meaning of death
- to help children develop a language for death and dying
- to give children the opportunity to develop strategies for coping when sad things happen

Possible materials

- flowers and dried flowers
- leaves and dried leaves
- seedpods, dried roots, bark, twigs
- a small animal skeleton
- seedless grapes and raisins
- tomatoes and sun-dried tomatoes

Ideas

1. Invite the children to feel all the objects in turn.

2. Encourage the use of all the senses – scrunching the dried leaves and listening to the noise, feeling the tickle of dried roots on the back of the hand, smelling the flowers, looking at the different shapes of the seedpods, feeling the different weights.

3. Ask the children to think about what all these objects have in common (e.g. nothing moves) and what differences there are (e.g. some are soft and can be bent, some are hard and rigid).

4. Ask the children to think about where the objects were found and whether they were always like they are now.

5. Invite the children to eat a grape and then a raisin. Encourage discussion of how they taste different.

6. Encourage the children to think about a cycle of life and the changes it involves, and ask them to consider how outside appearances alter.

7. Ask the children what the objects are like to touch and how the 'dead' objects feel different. Encourage them to explore different words for 'dead'.

8. Develop a discussion of what's different between when a person is there and when that person goes away or dies.

9. Encourage children to talk about how they remember people when they're separated from them.

10. Ask the children to think of something that reminds them of the person who they are not with.

11. End with a round of circle time inviting the children to share their memory with the class if they would like to.

12. Ensure that all children know how to get further support if they need it, and which teacher or classroom assistant they can talk to on a one-to-one basis.

Suggestions for a secondary school activity

Intentions

- to help students explore loss and change
- to explore different circumstances in which loss happens
- to explore different levels of loss
- to give the opportunity to develop listening skills and re-examine personal beliefs

Ideas

1. Begin by asking students to think of different kinds of loss. This can mean different things to different people and possible losses might include: death of a family member/friend/pet, a relationship break-up, parents' divorce, exam failure, job interview failure, theft, mugging, rape, discovery of adoption, end of friendship, abortion, infertility, becoming disabled.

2. Ask students to create value statements out of these – for example, 'Losing eyesight would be worse than losing hearing' or 'Parents separating is not as bad as one of them dying' (see the Possible statements for debate below for further ideas).

3. Ask students to mark each statement with 'Agree', 'Disagree' or 'Don't Know'.

4. Request a volunteer to pick one statement and argue for or against it.

5. Ask the rest of the class to listen, to be prepared to change their views, and then vote for or against the speaker.

6. Ask the class to consider whether their initial decision changed or remained unchanged.

7. Encourage the students to discuss the fact that we all have prejudices.

8. Use the debate to reflect that it's good to respect other people's views and not to judge others' experiences based on our own.

Possible statements for debate

1. Miscarriage is an easier loss to deal with than a baby or child dying as families will have fewer memories.

2. Expected death through illness is easier to deal with than sudden death through accident.

3. Being disabled from birth is easier than becoming disabled.

4. Older people get over death more easily than younger people because they are more used to it.

5. Pets can be replaced so owners shouldn't be sad when they die.

6. Parents' divorce is easier to cope with than one parent's death.

Support Groups

These are listed in alphabetical order with website addresses only as other contact details can change more frequently.

UK

BACP (British Association of Counselling and Psychotherapy)
www.bacp.co.uk
Information on counselling and psychotherapy in the UK.

Bereaved Parents Network
www.careforthefamily.org.uk/bpn
Support for parents who have lost a child (Christian but open to all faiths and none).

British Institute of Learning Disabilities
www.bild.org.uk
Provides books that explain death and bereavement to children with learning disabilities.

Cancerbacup
www.cancerbacup.org.uk
Up-to-date cancer information, practical advice and support for cancer patients, their families and carers.

Child Bereavement UK
www.childbereavement.org.uk
Support and resources for all those affected both when a child dies and when a child is bereaved.

Child Death Helpline
www.childdeathhelpline.org.uk
A freephone service for all those affected by the death of a child – not a counselling service.

Childhood Bereavement Network
www.childhoodbereavementnetwork.org.uk
Information, guidance and support services for bereaved children, their families and carers.

Childline
www.childline.org.uk
Free national helpline for children and young people in need of help or counselling.

The Compassionate Friends (UK)
www.tcf.org.uk
Support for bereaved parents and their families when a child has died.

Cruse Bereavement Care Youth Line RD4U
www.rd4u.org.uk
A website for children and young people aged between 12 and 18 who have been bereaved.

Grief Encounter
www.griefencounter.com
Helping bereaved children and young people rebuild their lives after a family death.

The Lullaby Trust
www.lullabytrust.org.uk
Support for families bereaved by Sudden Infant Death Syndrome.

Miscarriage Association

www.miscarriageassociation.org.uk

Support and information for those suffering the effects of pregnancy loss.

Samaritans

www.samaritans.org

A confidential listening service.

Sands (Stillbirth and neonatal death charity)

www.uk-sands.org

Support for parents who experience the loss of a baby during or after the birth.

Shooting Star Chase

www.shootingstarchase.org.uk

Support for babies, children and young people with life-limiting conditions and their families.

Together for Short Lives

www.togetherforshortlives.org.uk

Support and information for all children with life-threatening and life-limiting conditions and all those who love and care for them.

Winston's Wish

www.winstonswish.org

Support, information and guidance for bereaved children, young people and for those caring for bereaved families.

USA

Griefwatch

www.griefwatch.com

Offers spiritual, emotional and other support to children and adults who are grieving.

Kidsaid

www.kidsaid.com

A safe place to deal with feelings and for parents and kids to ask questions.

Rainbows

www.rainbows.org

Emotional healing for children grieving a loss from a life-altering crisis.

WinterSpring

www.winterspring.org

Enabling kids to develop healthy coping skills that will serve them throughout their lives.

Australia and New Zealand

Bereaved by Suicide

www.bereavedbysuicide.com.au

Support and resources for children and families bereaved by suicide.

Kidshealth

www.kidshealth.org.nz

Information about children and grief under the topic 'Bereavement Reactions'.

Skylight

www.skylight.org.nz

Support for people of all ages who are facing a tough life situation of change, loss, trauma or grief.

by the same author

What Does Dead Mean?
A Book for Young Children to Help Explain Death and Dying
Caroline Jay and Jenni Thomas
Illustrated by Unity-Joy Dale
ISBN 978 1 84905 355 6
eISBN 978 0 85700 705 6

also published by Jessica Kingsley Publishers

Talking with Children and Young People about Death and Dying
2nd edition
Mary Turner
Illustrated by Bob Thomas
ISBN 978 1 84310 441 4
eISBN 978 1 84642 560 8

Children Also Grieve
Talking about Death and Healing
Linda Goldman
ISBN 978 1 84310 808 5
eISBN 978 1 84642 471 7

Helping Children to Cope with Change, Stress and Anxiety
A Photocopiable Activities Book
Deborah M. Plummer
Illustrated by Alice Harper
ISBN 978 1 84310 960 0
eISBN 978 0 85700 366 9

Ladybird's Remarkable Relaxation
How children (and frogs, dogs, flamingos and dragons) can use yoga relaxation
to help deal with stress, grief, bullying and lack of confidence
Michael Chissick
Illustrated by Sarah Peacock
ISBN 978 1 84819 146 4
eISBN 978 0 85701 112 1

Talking About Death and Bereavement in School
How to Help Children Aged 4 to 11 to Feel Supported and Understood
Ann Chadwick
ISBN 978 1 84905 246 7
eISBN 978 0 85700 527 4

Communicating with Children When a Parent is at the End of Life
Rachel Fearnley
ISBN 978 1 84905 234 4
eISBN 978 0 85700 475 8

Grandad's Ashes
Walter Smith
ISBN 978 1 84310 517 6
eISBN 978 1 84642 605 6

'Twixt Bay & Burn'

A History of Helen's Bay & Crawfordsburn

Bayburn Historical Society

Contents

Foreword   3

Chapter 1 – The Beginnings

Introduction   4
Geology and Pre-History   4
Sixteenth and Seventeenth Centuries   7
Maps, Rent Rolls and Other Sources   9
The Ballydavey Massacre –
26 January 1642   17
The Old Inn, Crawfordsburn   19

Chapter 2 – The Development of Helen's Bay and Crawfordsburn

The Clandeboye Contribution   25
The Belfast and County Down Railway –
'Every Creeping Thing'   31
Other Forms of Transport   34

Chapter 3 – Farming and Business Life in Former Times

The Rural Scene   37
In the Two Villages   46

Chapter 4 – Schools

Schools in the Two Villages   52
Nearby Schools   55
Sunday Schools and Other
Children's Organisations   58

Chapter 5 – Growing up in Crawfordsburn and Helen's Bay

A Range of Reminiscences   61

Chapter 6 – The Churches

The Beginnings – the Presbyterian Church
at Ballygilbert   72
Helen's Bay Presbyterian Church   73
Church of St John Baptist, Helen's Bay   78

Chapter 7 – In the Wars

Grey Point Fort   83
Recollections of Colonel Bertram Cotton   88
Wartime Recollections of Jim Page   91
The Home Front including Helen's Bay
Home Guard and Volunteers in
Crawfordsburn   91
My Wartime Memories by
Kathleen Davis   95
The POW Camp at Rockport   96

Chapter 8 – The Social Fabric

The Bayburn Historical Society   99
Fifty Years of Brownies in the Bay   99
Crawfordsburn Country Club   100
Helen's Bay Golf Club   105
Helen's Bay Lawn Tennis Club   107
Crawfordsburn and Helen's Bay –
Masonic Order   108
Crawfordsburn and Helen's Bay –
Orange Lodge   109
Helen's Bay Players   109
Helen's Bay Police Station   111
The Royal British Legion   112
Scout Camp at Crawfordsburn
Country Park   114
St John's Badminton Club   115
Yachting   116

Chapter 9 – The Sharman Crawfords of Crawfordsburn House

William Sharman Crawford   118
The Sharman Crawford Children   122
The later Sharman Crawfords   123

Chapter 10 – Personal Perspectives and other Notables

The Brown Family – a Glance into
the Past   128
Down our Way by 'Rene Shuttleworth   129
Helen's Bay Remembered by Jim Page   131
Craigdarragh House – Workman Family   133
Sir Crawford McCullagh of Rust Hall   134
Coastguards and Customs   134
George Best in Helen's Bay   136

Chapter 11 – The Ratepayers Association

Local History from the Minutes of
the Association   137

Chapter 12 – Natural History and Other Aspects of Local Interest

Crawfordsburn Country Park   144
Flora and Fauna   146
The Butterflies of Helen's Bay
and Crawfordsburn   146
The Crawfordsburn Fern   147
Local Weather   148

Bibliography and Further Reading   150

Acknowledgements   151